Untold Verses

The Bard

To you, my reader,

I hope you resonate with a piece of this humble
bard's rhymes.

Foreword

This is a collection of emotions filled with words... on human intellect, influence and intrigues.

The world we experience at present is filled with myriad shades of emotions...
Outbursts on communalism... Sentiments on inhumane attitudes...
Blatant articulations on injustice unfolded in society....
Blushes and frustrations on sensitive issues...
Brutal voicing up over endangering manipulations...
Bare utterances on the need of the hour...

And also…

Appreciations on social cohesiveness, humanity, sensitisation rather than sensationalization..

And it is definitely a fact that language can portray a variety of responses on numerous value points.
An open intellect with even a handful of words can powerfully present the social scenario in its poetic canvas.

This is the birth of a bard.. who muses over language and interprets the panoramic world at the fingertips...
Ink flows into paper in beautifully carved out images...
Words become daggers..
They slit open the dark truths of reality.
They cut into edges...
They marvel in portrayals...

The words..
They make you think deep.
They force you to a halt.
They let you envisage and reconnect...
They drag you out from your cozy cocoon
to the heat of the day...
They make you ponder over the way out..
The way out to recreate..
To redo things...
To reciprocate...
To rekindle your intellect..

And thus, if not to pen and proclaim... at least..
to clasp your hands with the world in need...

And thus...
Be one among them..
A saviour stretching your mighty hand..

Be the shade...
Be the armour...
Be what the world needs..
Because, the Almighty has endowed you in abundance.

The musings penned here are worth a lifetime.
They do not fancy things..
They sketch the world in its gross sheets.
We get a remarkable threading of carefully crafted words into
a real life scenario.

The bard.. the poet has finished off a marvellous work of
discourse.

A must read...
A poke into our intellect.
A beautiful one at that.

Best wishes…

"No writer dares make changes in the foreword"
                                        - Sajeda P F

Deception

Contents

Narrative

The embers turned into a fire.
It started gnawing at my conscience from the
inside.
The rise of casteist riots and public humiliation
minorities were being subjected to, in my
country, was unbearable.
A land that was once a symbol of unity in
diversity, now spreads hate like wildfire.

Divide

Once upon a time,
In a nation full of pride,
Rich with people far and wide,
United by echoes of freedom's chime,
Differences set aside, we stood side by side.

Oh, the tale is now so old,
And a divide hidden does linger,
The peace we sought slowly wither,
For our hearts once warm now turn cold,
Poisoned by slithering men's blither.

Parts of a whole now torn apart,
Hate takes form, the whisperer their guide,
Numb fools spill blood with each stride,
Their conscience a lost art,
They birth genocide.

Narrative

I must start this one with how smitten I am by
my home, coined 'Shade' by my mother.
A beautiful piece of lush green paradise, veiled
by ivory fences and a once ebony gate, coveting
an undoubtedly large variety of flora.
Again, the tiny forest and our settlement,
be it its design or implementation, are
the fruits of my mother's eccentric brain.
Among a few spots we cherish,
disconnecting us from the burdens of the
mundane world,
is the hammock under the bilimbi tree, with but
of course,
diverse shades of green bilimbis hanging from
the rather light bark,
with a canopy of alternately arranged ovate
leaflets.
Well, I was lying there and it got me thinking of
how beautiful God's creations
are, except maybe us humans, when we choose
not to be.

The Bilimbi Tree

I lay there in a hammock under the bilimbi tree,
A book on my belly, my mind wandering free.

The leaves waltzed with gentle zephyrs,
And a radiant sun streaking through the lush
canopy,
Had me ponder what we've all turned out to be.
Why are we billions, adorned with a million
pyres?
For now, past the green, a gloomy grey is all I
see.

Ye, our greed has consumed us whole,
A creed that now condemns a moral soul.

Narrative

I'm a rather strong believer on how people can't
resist meddling in just about everything their
impish hands can reach.
Surely, their arrogance pollutes anything and
everything, except maybe one thing, my faith
and let's not get into that now.

The poem 'Ozymandias' and the sonnet 'Not
marble nor the gilded monuments', have always
been something that stuck to me, since I learnt it
in school.
This is my frail attempt at
taking a jab at the society, that interferes
in everyone else's life, but their own,
ravaging true identities and rendering lives
futile and lifeless.
This extends to much more but, certainly not
excluding the material.

A Rhyme for Ages

Herein I ink a memoir for ages,
A verse to trump over that of fools for sages.

Let the words that misled you leave its stain,
And guide you in times when your heart's slain.
To the countless you played with your lies,
Open your eyes and own your heart's cries.

Alone we must thrive as this simple a rhyme,
Unruffled by no mortal nor one as savage as
time.

Narrative

Have you ever stepped back from the strong
currents of trend driven crowds
and observed their lust for anything marketed
as pop culture?
Ever felt like our lives are directed by
something?
I can't deny I haven't constantly been poked by
this thought, every time I traverse the media.
Most definitely, their algorithms are simply
the new way of catering to the many desires
blossoming in minds, young and old.
Ask the latter, they'll proclaim how there's
always been those who exploit.
They were few then, so were those who resisted
them.

Orchestra Of Life

Noises enshroud our ears,
they lead us, our visions blinded,
And with the power of countless fears,
puppeteered are we, with strings of hatred.

For cryptic rights and wrongs, we fight,
our thoughts directed, truths forfeit,
Unaware of the murk veiled in their light,
We tread paths lit by lamps of deceit.

Narrative

If these verses need narration, I beg of you to
think with the brain you've been gifted.
It's soul rending how the beautiful children,
people – young and old,
are tormented and tortured without remorse or
reason.
Why have we let this go on?
Have you not seen wailing babies with lost
limbs, crying over their dead mothers, and
maimed torn mothers searching rubbles for their
own?
Do you turn your eyes and heart the other way
when they stand strong, though they're
relentlessly hammered with gunfire and
bombing?
Have they subjugated you so much that you can
no longer think and act for yourself?
Are you not an individual with thoughts, body
and a soul of your own?
Act, human.

For Palestine

You whose hearts to the devil's been sold,
What's in you that has no cure?
That you must lie and abuse and leave bodies
cold,
Your pharisaic hearts', twisted and impure.

An eerie silence hides among endless wails,
A murky presence now looms over the brightest
days,
Bloodied thousands await answers to their
desolate hails,
Helpless, the world looks to the divine, devoid
of a face.

Beware, you who feast on the true and innocent,
Of retribution that'll hunt your evil scent.

Disruption

Smothered souls watch their homes bombed
down,
Sired by the fetish of a vile genocidal crown.

The voices of millions hammered by their
selfish frowns,
Their forked tongues mask pleas as devilish
sounds.

Pretence

Ignorance breeds their false sanctimony,
Indeed, their fires rage on sans humanity,
Aware and shameless, we covet our frail
comfort,
And in flocks we follow the words of an unseen
bigot.

Gazan plea

Ye mundane who jest that you be selfless,
'Yond mountains and raging seas,
Why do we all act so hopelessly helpless?
Wails and cries echo unto our ears
useless,
Withal they shamelessly enact plays of
pretentious peace.

For those that shout without reason,
For their hearts like voices, changes with
season.

Narrative

The night sky adorned with a plethora of stars
and
a stark crescent, is a beautiful sight to behold.
Yet, when the lights go out, in the bleak
moonlight that falls upon the land,
there creeps a darkness in the hearts of men and
women.
It's not as if the day is much better now, but the
blankets of nights have always been notorious.
For what's unseen is easier to pass off as that
which never happened.

Inversion

Life evermore wild and loud at night,
Khonsu soars with a malevolent smile,
A world astray slumbers in Khepri's light,
Lies veiled as candour, pile in hearts vile.

Narrative

Ah, India is a beautiful country,
be it the gorgeous variety of ecosystems
or the people that welcome you with warm
hearts. But like yin and yang there's another
side to them.
The poor conditions of minorities were often
caused by the ignorance of the privileged.
With the huge population, the medics often had
to work tirelessly and help those in need to the
best of their abilities.
More often than not, owing to the limited
facilities in government hospitals.

Be that as it may, the helped, often cloud their
intellects by rushes of emotions for their
beloved. This gave rise to a despicable side in
them that did deplorable things.
Be grateful and hopeful, not arrogant and
ignorant, my brothers and sisters. A gentle
subtle reminder that without their help most of
us would not have made it this far.

Ode to the Medics

Oi proud emotive human, have you not a brain?
Are you not different, for you can think?
Why, when you run to them writhing in pain,
do they nurture you to be put in the drain?
How much farther can your humanity sink?

Do you not see their sleepless nights and
endless days?
Their breathless crusades to save lives that
fade?
Retainers of fatigued bodies and denied pays.
They travail unmindful of your ignorant ways,
For they're aware of the thousands that
decayed.

One day, you'll cling by a thread to your life,
Even then, they don't succumb to ignorance.
So, be kind to the saviours in their strife.
What if you get what you served, in resonance?

Narrative

Why are humans obsessed with causing strife
and grief amidst their own?
I can't ever understand what comes out of using
another for their own desires.
How long will their pleasure last?
Why would you leave another weak, clueless
and broken,
for mere moments of satisfaction?
Aye, call it my curse.. but, retribution is a bill
that's never overdue.

The Wronged

Herein I ink an eternal memoir,
Of not one heart or two, but a full foyer.

Let it be etched in your hearts, ye wrongful,
The filthy stain from those you left woeful.

Humans we are and mistakes we make,
Alas cometh the hour, waver not to wake.

For the ravages of time can leave you unwhole,
With no one left to answer your call.

Narrative

We were ten, till the angel chose to return and then we were nine, destined to mourn.

Until we are reunited again, I hope we live lives worthy of having been blessed by your presence.

Ode to the Fallen

The seven skies turn a grim shade,
To red barren earth, we let you fade.
I watched you disintegrate, but rather,
Have waited forever, than lose you, my
brother.

Take heed! For every soul shall be lent a taste,
The eternal beauty of the end, make no haste.

For your time too will come, it simply must,
like a brewing storm to a ravaging gust.
You'll live on in ten breaths,
every blink, till we join you in our deaths.

Narrative

Past the towering Himalayas,
over the scorching Thar and boasting viridian
forests,
amidst two oceans, lies a land of diverse
brainwashed people that's forgotten unity.
They now crave disparity fueled by hate
immense
and an obvious lack of wisdom.

Unite

To the young and those aged gold,
Let not your hearts be biased and cold,
Bring down barricades that set us apart,
For we're all no more than a beating heart.

I pray don't give into hate,
Oh, unite and reforge our fate,
Let's calm our minds, the many and the few,
And let love blossom anew.

Neo-Patriotism

Wailing souls swooped away by holy
fires,
The lands now brim of hatred and
divine liars.

Narrative

Let not our bodies be marionettes guided by
strings of the devil.
Let not those craving powers poison your souls
that yearn to love.

Marionettes

Why are lives left to waste?
Why do we succumb to so much hate?
The strings of the evil move us, with love for
none,
Till we march again, mindless of our faiths, as
one.

Move not your hearts for the whispers of
slithering men,
May not your words be guided by propaganda's
pen.
For if our creeds bring us apart and not together,
Fiendish they've become, rewritten forever.

Narrative

By now you might have been led to assume that
this writer hates humans.
I most certainly do not. I cherish them.
I admire how each of their brains work
differently and
come up with the most amazing ideas and,
oh! the number of perspectives they conjure,
truly miraculous.
Yet, given such a beautiful gift to think and
perceive
we use it to subjugate, manipulate and satisfy
our unending thirst,
for simply more than what we have.
Even the goal is indefinite yet they seek to
satisfy it, truly funny, isn't it?
The species that can come up with the most
innovative inventions and solutions, blind to the
most obvious ones.
Perhaps it's my perspective that's different, but I
have absolutely no intention of joining a herd
grazing fenced grass.

Mundane

Centuries filled and fuelled by greed,
Crooked is our tale stretched through time,
Divided yet bound by lethe, the mundane breed,
Drenched in hymns as old as brine.

Muse

Forced to breathe in a deceitful world,
We dream foolish to the likes of
Akator's gold.

Human imprisonment

We tread in many shades of shackled
deceptive freedom,
And voice like imbeciles for directed
hammered wisdom.

Apiary

With lies controlling lives,
We are subject to slavery of hives.

Narrative

There was a time when I'd given my trust to
someone,
whom I thought was oppressed and in need of
it.
So, I ignored my instincts and after repeated
imposition, I decided to give it a chance.
I try my best to not ignore my instincts after
that, but I lost myself.
I thought I had to if I had to help them no matter
what.
As long as I could get them out of the prison
they said they were in.
Turns out, some are prisoned for a reason.

Relic

Aye every blink ever since we met,
I wished for the sun to never set.

Now lost in an abyss of lies,
I wander amidst my heart's cries.

They echo through a thousand years,
And I let out hope's endless tears.

Deep in the dark I must hide,
Never can I be by your side.

Alas my dreams journey unto you,
So, with reality, I'm fed up and through.

Every day, breath by breath, I die,
A tortured soul without a reason why.

Narrative

I am blessed with a comfortable life.
It haunts me everyday that I do not help enough.
Knowing that there are people out there that
could use my help,
no matter how little that might be.
Perhaps, what's little for me is a lot for many.
My soul is often heavy with the sin of living
without worries,
whilst they barely have food for a penny.
Some that can't wish for water to quench, much
less than the luxury of meals.
I would be delusional to think that all live
comfortably,
when there's constant domination wrought by
those that hold power.

Sin of Silence

Counting my cornucopia of blessings,
Covering my regret in shame's drapings.
For posh desires and a journey of impulses,
Forever a debt to the price of their fleeting
pulses.

Every breath in my comforts now feel sinful
and perjured,
Every boon He ever gifted, a test of charity I've
conjured.

Dear reader,

I thank you for sharing this journey with me.
Indeed, it was a short one but I hope you enjoyed it.
Until next time...
I pray we meet again soon.

With Love,
The Bard